Jekyll & Hyde

The Musical

Cover Illustration by Serino, Coyne, Inc.
Production photography by Cylla Von Tiedemann

The original Broadway cast recording
of *Jekyll & Hyde The Musical* is available on
Atlantic Theatre/Atlantic Records
(82976-2-CD)

Visit our website at www.cherrylane.com

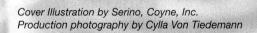

Photos: Title Page: "Confrontation": Robert Cuccioli as Henry Jekyll and Edward Hyde. This page and next: Jekyll in the laboratory (center). Insets: above, Jekyll and Emma (Christiane Noll); opposite page, Hyde and his first victim (top); "Murder, Murder!" (middle); "It's A Dangerous Game": Lucy (Linda Eder) and Hyde (bottom).

Photos: Clockwise: "Façade"; "In His Eyes";
Jekyll in the lab (Robert Evan as Jekyll);
"Someone Like You."

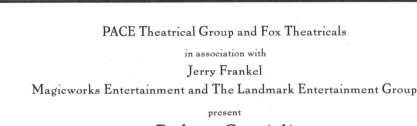

PACE Theatrical Group and Fox Theatricals
in association with
Jerry Frankel
Magicworks Entertainment and The Landmark Entertainment Group
present

Robert Cuccioli
Linda Eder
in

Jekyll & Hyde

Conceived for the stage by Steve Cuden and Frank Wildhorn

Book and Lyrics by   Music by

Leslie Bricusse   Frank Wildhorn

From the novella "The Strange Case of Dr. Jekyll and Mr. Hyde" by Robert Louis Stevenson.
Previous developmental productions by Alley Theatre, 5th Avenue Musical Theatre and Theatre Under The Stars.

also starring **Christiane Noll**
featuring **George Merritt, Robert Evan** and **Barrie Ingham**

with Geoffrey Blaisdell   David Chaney   Bill E. Dietrich   John Treacy Egan   Donald Grody

Paul Hadobas   Leah Hocking   Michael Ingram   David Koch   Frank Mastrone

Raymond Jaramillo McLeod   Brad Oscar   Molly Scott Pesce   Bonnie Schon   Emily Scott Skinner

Rebecca Spencer   Jodi Stevens   Martin Van Treuren   Charles E. Wallace   Emily Zacharias

Scenic Design	Costume Design	Lighting Design	Properties and Set Dressing
Robin Phillips	Ann Curtis	Beverly Emmons	Christina Poddubiuk
With			
James Noone			

Sound Design	Orchestrations	Musical Supervisor
Karl Richardson & Scott Stauffer	Kim Scharnberg	Jeremy Roberts

Musical Director	Vocal Arrangements	Music Coordinator
Jason Howland	Jason Howland & Ron Melrose	John Miller

Special Effects Design	Wig Design	Fight Coordinator	Production Stage Manager
Gregory Meeh	Paul Huntley	J. Allen Suddeth	Maureen F. Gibson

Associate Producer	General Management	Casting	Public Relations
Bill Young	Niko Associates	Julie Hughes & Barry Moss, C.S.A.	Richard Kornberg & Associates

Executive Producer	Choreography
Gary Gunas PACE Theatrical Group	Joey Pizzi

Directed by

Robin Phillips

Original Alley Theatre Production Directed by **Gregory Boyd**.

Virgin Atlantic Airways is the official airline of *Jekyll & Hyde*.

Infiniti is the official luxury automoblie of *Jekyll & Hyde*.

www.jekyll-hyde.com

14....Lost In The Darkness

16....Façade

28....Take Me As I Am

32....No One Knows Who I Am

36....Good And Evil

41....This Is The Moment

46....Alive!

49....Sympathy, Tenderness

52....Someone Like You

58....Murder, Murder!

72....Once Upon A Dream

75....In His Eyes

80....It's A Dangerous Game

87....A New Life

94....Confrontation

7....The Making of *Jekyll & Hyde*

9.... A Note From Composer Frank Wildhorn

10....Song and Story Outline

The Making of

Jekyll & HYDE

by Leslie Bricusse
Librettist and Lyricist

I was introduced to Frank Wildhorn on March 8, 1988. Our first musical collaboration, *Jekyll & Hyde*, opened on Broadway on April 28, 1997—nine years and change later.

To adapt Robert Louis Stevenson's remarkable 1886 novella into a stage musical had been Frank's dream since his college days at the University of Southern California—an idea so terrific and yet so obvious that I marveled that no one had ever thought of it before. Maybe they had, but it had certainly never got as far as the stage—and most certainly not as far as between 44th and 46th Streets, between Broadway and Eighth Avenue in New York City—the acknowledged center of the known Musical Theatre Universe.

It all began in a carefree enough manner. I was instantly enamored of Frank's music—richly theatrical melodies set in an exciting contemporary style—and writing the first draft was, comparatively speaking, a walk in the park. I set to work eagerly on the book. A strong story line soon emerged, and Frank and I promptly pounced upon the powerful song opportunities it offered. Across that first summer, which now seems as long ago as the dark Victorian era in which Henry Jekyll first embarked upon his legendary exploration into the duality of man, we wrote a first draft of some 20 songs, while incorporating a substantial quantity of recitative into the play. Little did we know at that early stage that our journey was destined to be certainly longer and almost as tortuous as Jekyll's—except that we have emerged, a near-decade later, alive and with a happy ending.

The reaction to our work was immediate and encouraging. Everyone realized what Frank and I had known from Day One—that we could write pretty good songs together. The best response came from singers. We had lunch one day in London with Sammy Davis, Jr. and Liza Minnelli, and afterwards played them "This Is The Moment" and "A New Life," which they each respectively claimed as their own. A few weeks later, when we were all together in Hawaii for Christmas, they became the first singing stars to perform these songs in public.

The Broadway ball started, if not exactly rolling, at least moving perceptibly forward. There was even talk, thanks to Frank's power-plant energy and enthusiasm, of a New York production as early as the spring of 1989. Wiser heads prevailed, making it 1990. Wiser heads still proposed a regional tryout first, which is why we all found ourselves at the Alley Theatre in Houston in the early spring of 1990.

Stylishly directed by the Alley's Gregory Boyd, the show was an instantaneous success there, with the theatre-going public lapping it up, faults and all. Its run was extended three or four times across the summer, creating an immediate cult following, both for the show and its shining new star, Linda Eder.

Paradoxically, one of the biggest, most unlikely and almost insurmountable problems that *Jekyll & Hyde* has faced has been that from the very beginning it smelled of success. It was in fact full of flaws, as most first draft shows are, but what *did* work worked *so* well that people came back to see it five, ten, and twenty times. The term "Jekkies" was coined to describe the die-hard fan club that has supported the show from that day to this. (A young lady who works for a major airline told me last week she had seen the show 43 times in 22 cities!)

So instead of undergoing the normal *(normal?)*, sane-as-anything-ever-can-be-in-a-musical process of gradual rewriting and refining, we were pounced on by a bevy of check-waving, wanna-be entrepreneurs, most of whose "Broadway" producing experience was at best a nodding acquaintance with the legit box-office grosses in *Variety*. Because of *Jekyll & Hyde*'s sensational audience response, these almost Runyonesque characters were swift to sniff our dollar potential. They started to pull *Jekyll & Hyde* in 14 different directions at once, like a litter of puppies attacking a rug, in their fevered attempts to get a piece of what they sensed would be the action.

The problem was accentuated by the fact that the ever-resourceful Frank had parlayed RCA Records in *London*—God knows how!—into making a major concept album of our first draft score, starring Colm Wilkinson of *Les Miserables* and *Phantom Of The Opera* fame, as Jekyll and Hyde, in tandem with our treasured leading lady, Linda Eder. The record, too, was an instant success. It sold amazingly well for an unknown show, and the songs started to be performed on radio and television—especially "This Is The Moment," which overnight seemed to become the anthem for every form of televised competition from Miss America to the Winter Olympics to the Superbowl to the World Series. Its notoriety became almost embarrassing, with theatre critics relishing the cheap-shot opportunity to pick it off as "ice-rink music."

All of the above factors somehow combined to lead us on to a bizarre and seemingly endless Yellow Brick Road, presided over by too many chieftains and not enough Indians, that wound its twisted way from a spectacular regional success via a wretchedly misconceived nightmare New York workshop and a mind-numbing two-year legal deadlock to a money-making but still-far-from-perfect national tour.

The highlight of this otherwise desultory half-decade came in 1994 when the irrepressible Frank convinced Atlantic Records that this was the perfect moment in time to make the *second* recording of the by now two-and-a-half hour score of our still unproduced Broadway show—this time a *double* CD concept album, which he, Frank, would produce and they, Atlantic, would release on the to-be-created Atlantic Theatre label, which they, Atlantic, would form and he, Frank, would run for them! Amazingly, and at vast expense, all this came to pass, and the resultant product went on to become an even bigger success than its RCA predecessor!

The Yellow Brick Road finally went full circle, and in January, 1995, there we were again back in our by-now-beloved Houston, this time at the 3,000-seat Music Hall. Once again, as in a recurring dream, Houston audiences went mad for *Jekyll & Hyde*, to the show-stopping tune of millions of box-office dollars.

Finally, in 1997, in the finest tradition of Yellow Brick Roads, ours has led us to the Emerald City of Broadway. Thanks to the patience and abiding faith in *Jekyll & Hyde* of our longtime supporters and now Broadway producers, the Pace Theatrical Group, from guess where?—that's right, Houston!—and Fox Theatricals from Atlanta, we have at long, long last crossed over from the Yellow Brick Road to the Great White Way. We were quintuply blessed to have this new and definitive production designed and directed by the remarkable talents of Robin Phillips, and starring the three most dazzling new musical theatre talents, I venture to suggest, to arrive on Broadway in many a season—Robert Cuccioli, Linda Eder, and Christiane Noll.

Future productions of *Jekyll & Hyde* are already in the works for a dozen countries around the world—including Australia, Germany, Sweden, Denmark, Canada, England, and the Benelux countries.

And best of all—wouldn't you know?—a smiling Frank Wildhorn is, at the time of this writing, happily producing the show's *third* CD. It is that most coveted of all recordings for every composer and lyricist—the original Broadway cast album!

Leslie Bricusse

Saint-Paul de Vence
June 2, 1997

A Note From Composer
Frank Wildhorn

I can't believe we're finally here. After the longest pregnancy I could ever imagine, *Jekyll & Hyde* is on Broadway. I never thought I would produce this score three times in seven years, and it is a testament to those who have worked so hard for so long and those who have never lost faith that we are here.

I will forever be in debt and filled with honor and gratitude to Karl Richardson, Kim Scharnberg, and Jeremy Roberts, who have been my partners on all three *Jekyll & Hyde* recordings. It has also been a real thrill for me to watch Jason Howland pick up the baton given to him by Kim and watch him lead the orchestra.

From London, Miami, and Canada to Los Angeles and New York, from a wonderful group of actors and studio singers to my amazing "original" cast of the Broadway show, from Gregory Boyd, who gave so many of us our first shot, and the Alley theatre through the workshops and our national tour to the captain of our ship, Robin Phillips, here on Broadway, from Colm Wilkinson to Chuck Wagner to Terry Mann to Anthony Warlow to Bob Cuccioli, from Rebecca Spencer to Carolee Carmello to Christiane Noll, it has been the most remarkable musical journey of my life. And to Linda Eder, whose glorious voice this piece was written for and whose performances of these songs Leslie and I created have given them the "best of all possible lives," I am as always filled with admiration and so much love.

Shows don't just happen, they are produced. So, to the producers my heartfelt gratitude: to Allen and Shirley Becker, to Brian Becker, to Miles and Connie Wilkin, to Scott and Kathy Zeiger, and to Lee Marshall, David Fay, Mick Leavitt, Tony Christopher, and

Jerry Frankel. And I must include an extra heartfelt thank you to Gary Gunas who has lived and breathed and fought for the Broadway production with passion and class.

In the end, this show lives because of the audience for whom it was written, and it is you the fans that have stood by Leslie and I and shared this journey with us. We would not exist but for you, and forever you have our gratitude and love.

Enjoy! Keep the faith.

Jekyll & Hyde

Song & Story Outline

Act One

London, 1885. DR. HENRY JEKYLL, a brilliant young doctor and research scientist, anguishes over his father's inexplicable mental illness ("Lost In The Darkness"). Jekyll is obsessed by the belief that, given appropriate support by his peers in the medical profession, he can separate the dual elements of good and evil that are constantly struggling for supremacy inside every human being ("Façade").

Jekyll presents his case to the highly conservative and unsympathetic BOARD OF GOVERNORS of St. Jude's Mental Hospital. He needs to test his theories on a live human being. His request is unanimously and summarily rejected, except by the President of the Board, SIR DANVERS CAREW, Jekyll's future father-in-law, who abstains from voting. The rest of the Board dismiss Jekyll as a dangerous radical. Jekyll's closest friend and advisor, his lawyer JOHN UTTERSON, sympathizes.

The ill-feeling from that fateful encounter carries over into the evening at the glittering reception given by Sir Danvers to celebrate Jekyll's engagement to his daughter EMMA. Jekyll arrives late at the party, unrepentant. He tells Emma he is more determined than ever to pursue his course of action ("Take Me As I Am").

Utterson tries to take Jekyll's mind off his problems by dragging him unwillingly to a disreputable East End Dockland dive called "The Red Rat." Among the girls working at the club is LUCY HARRIS, a disillusioned young soul who wants to make something of her life ("No One Knows Who I Am"). On stage, Lucy displays a vibrant personality as she sings an appropriately decadent song ("Good And Evil"). Jekyll is incensed when the club's seedy owner, sinisterly know as THE SPIDER, physically abuses Lucy in front of the customers. Consoling her, Jekyll gives her his card, should she ever need a friend.

Returning home, Jekyll thanks Utterson for the dubious relaxation provided by "The Red Rat" visit. He decides to work late. He talks with POOLE, his butler, of his father's great qualities before his present dark illness descended on him. Jekyll's mind is made up ("This Is The Moment").

In his laboratory, Jekyll records in his journal that he is making himself the subject of his experiment. He injects himself with the prepared formula and is horrifyingly transformed into EDWARD HYDE. As Hyde, he exults in his new, evil and liberated persona ("Alive!").

Jekyll's experiments continue. He disappears from society and becomes reclusive, unavailable to even his closest circle—Emma, Utterson, Poole, Sir Danvers. They are unaware of the demons he is dealing with as he remains isolated and locked away in his laboratory.

Jekyll receives an unexpected visit from Lucy, who has been badly injured by a sadistic gentleman visitor to "The Red Rat." Jekyll is appalled, and tenderly treats her wounds. Lucy says she will never forget the man's name . . . "Hyde . . . Edward Hyde." Jekyll is transfixed with horror. He completes her treatment. Overwhelmed by his kindness, she kisses him, at first in gratitude, then in passion ("Sympathy, Tenderness"). A confused Jekyll takes his leave of her. Lucy daydreams of her impossible relationship with Jekyll as she wanders the streets of London ("Someone Like You").

Back in the seedier streets of London's Dockland, Hyde interrupts a sordid liaison between THE BISHOP OF BASINGSTOKE, one of the St. Jude's Hospital Board of Governors, and a teenage prostitute. Hyde batters the hypocritical cleric to death and sets fire to his body in a frenzy of rage. Hyde has become Jekyll's avenging angel of death.

Act Two

Hyde's rampage of killing continues as he systematically assassinates further members of the Board of Governors of St. Jude's Hospital ("Murder, Murder!"). By the end of it, five of them are dead.

Emma, frantic with worry about her fiancé, enters Jekyll's for-once-unlocked laboratory, looking for him. She sees and reads his journal. Jekyll returns and is furious at her intrusion. Unaware of the truth, she soothes and encourages him, trying to bring him back to the path of reason ("Once Upon A Dream"). She will wait for him, however long it takes.

Emma departs. Jekyll records in his journal that the experiment is out of control. Utterson arrives, deeply concerned over Jekyll's letter to him leaving everything he possesses to Hyde, should anything ill befall Jekyll. Jekyll persuades Utterson to continue to have faith in the experiments. Utterson goes in search of the drugs Jekyll desperately needs from the pharmacist to continue his struggle against Hyde.

Emma and Lucy separately and simultaneously sing of their deep but confused feelings for the man they both love ("In His Eyes").

Hyde comes to seek out Lucy. Disappointed, hoping against hope she will see Jekyll, Lucy is nonetheless irresistibly attracted to Hyde ("It's A Dangerous Game!").

Utterson returns to Jekyll's lab with the drugs from the pharmacist, to find Hyde waiting for him. Utterson refuses to give the drugs to anyone except Jekyll. Trapped, Hyde has no option other than to reveal himself to Utterson. He injects himself and reverts back to Jekyll before the horrified eyes of his friend. Jekyll gives him a farewell letter to Lucy, begging her to leave London at once. He believes that with the new drugs he can finally destroy Hyde. Utterson hurries away on his errand of mercy.

Utterson reads Jekyll's letter to the illiterate Lucy and beseeches her to do Jekyll's bidding and leave London with the money he has sent her, and start a new life elsewhere. Lucy, left alone, considers her frail future ("A New Life"). Hyde arrives and taunts Lucy for her relationship with Jekyll. Singing to her soothingly, he stabs her viciously to death as his voice rises to a frenzied pitch of fury.

Back in his lab, Jekyll knows he has entered the very gates of Hell. The voice of Hyde is now within him, and the two halves of his broken soul engage in a desperate final battle for supremacy ("Confrontation"). Jekyll trades Hyde blow for bitter blow, determined not to succumb to his evil alter ego.

And back from the edge of death he comes, to the sound of wedding bells. Jekyll stands at the altar, before an elegant congregation of friends, with his beautiful bride Emma at his side. As the wedding service begins, the evil spirit of Hyde wells up inside him yet once more and takes him over, to the horror of the assembled guests. Hyde claims victory—"There is no Henry Jekyll—only Edward Hyde!" Hyde strangles one of the guests and threatens to kill Emma. Emma speaks calmly to the Jekyll deep within Hyde, and knows he will not harm her. The Jekyll in Hyde hears her, and somehow finds the strength to let her go. Utterson unsheathes his swordstick. Hyde begs his old friend to end his suffering and set them all free. Utterson cannot do it. Hyde runs on to his sword and falls, mortally wounded.

Emma cradles him in her arms. Jekyll's voice and persona return to him as his life slips away and he speaks his final word, "Emma . . ." She holds him close and comforts him . . . "Rest now, my tormented love," as he dies in her embrace.

Leslie Bricusse

Plymouth Theatre, New York
May 5, 1997

Leslie Bricusse

Book and Lyrics

Leslie Bricusse is a writer-composer-lyricist who has contributed to many musical films and plays during his career. He was born in London and educated at University College School and Gonville and Caius College, Cambridge. At Cambridge, he was President of the Footlights Revue Club and founded the Musical Comedy Club. There, he co-authored, directed and performed in his first two musical shows, *Out Of The Blue* and *Lady At The Wheel*, both of which made their way to London's West End. He also found time in the gaps to acquire a Master of Arts Degree.

The late, great Beatrice Lillie plucked him out of the Footlights Revue at the Phoenix Theatre, and made him her leading man in *An Evening With Beatrice Lillie* at the Globe Theatre, where he spent the first year of his professional life writing another musical, *Boy On The Corner*, and the screenplay and score of his first motion picture, *Charley Moon*, which won him his first Ivor Novello Award. That year he decided to drop the possibilities of directing and performing, and concentrate his career on becoming a full-time writer-composer-lyricist.

His subsequent stage musicals include *Stop The World—I Want To Get Off*; *The Roar Of The Greasepaint—The Smell Of The Crowd*; *Pickwick*; *Harvey*; *The Good Old Bad Old Days*; *Goodbye, Mr. Chips*; *Henry's Wives*; *Scrooge*; *One Shining Moment*; *Sherlock Holmes*; *Jekyll & Hyde*, and *Victor/Victoria*. He has written songs and/or screenplays for such films as *Doctor Dolittle*; *Scrooge*; *Willy Wonka And The Chocolate Factory*; *Goodbye, Mr. Chips*; *Superman*; *Victor/Victoria*; *Santa Claus—The Movie*; *Home Alone* and *Home Alone 2*; *Hook*; *Tom & Jerry—The Movie*, and various *Pink Panther* films.

Bricusse has written more than 40 musical shows and films, and over the years has had the good fortune to enjoy fruitful collaborations with a wonderful array of musical talents including Anthony Newley, Henry Mancini, John Williams, John Barry, Jerry Goldsmith, Jule Styne, André Previn, Frank Wildhorn, and Peter Illyich Tchaikovsky (whose *Nutcracker Suite* he adapted into a song score).

His better-known songs include "What Kind Of Fool Am I?," "Once In A Lifetime," "Gonna Build A Mountain," "Who Can I Turn To?," "The Joker," "If I Ruled The World," "My Kind Of Girl," "Talk To The Animals," "You And I," "Feeling Good," "When I Look In Your Eyes," "Goldfinger," "Can You Read My Mind?" (the love theme from *Superman*), "You Only Live Twice," "Le Jazz Hot!," "On A Wonderful Day Like Today," "Two For The Road," "The Candy Man," "This Is The Moment," and "Crazy World."

He has been nominated for ten Academy Awards, eight Grammys, and four Tonys, and has won two Oscars, a Grammy and eight Ivor Novello Awards, the premier British music award. In 1989 he received the Kennedy Award for consistent excellence in British Songwriting, bestowed by the British Academy of Songwriters, Composers and Authors. The same year he was inducted into the American Songwriters' Hall Of Fame in New York—only the fourth Englishman to be so honoured, after Noël Coward, John Lennon, and Paul McCartney.

Bricusse is currently represented on Broadway by *Victor/Victoria*, which has successively starred Julie Andrews, Liza Minnelli and Raquel Welch, on which he collaborated with Blake Edwards and Henry Mancini, and *Jekyll & Hyde*, which recently completed a nationwide U.S. tour prior to its Broadway opening in spring of 1997. Bricusse's next project is a stage musical of *Doctor Dolittle*, and is scheduled to open in London in the summer of 1998.

Frank Wildhorn

Music

Frank Wildhorn is a composer-lyricist/producer/creator whose works span the worlds of popular theatrical and classical music. He is currently represented on Broadway with *Jekyll & Hyde*, written with Leslie Bricusse and directed by Robin Phillips. Wildhorn also contributed to the Henry Mancini/Leslie Bricusse musical hit, *Victor/Victoria*. At this writing, Wildhorn's next Broadway show, *The Scarlet Pimpernel*, written with Nan Knighton, is scheduled to open on Broadway in the fall of 1997.

Also in pre-production at this time is *The Civil War—An American Musical*. Written with Jack Murphy and Gregory Boyd, this musical will be performed on a national tour, preceded by a two-hour televised concert of the show's score and the release of a star-studded double CD concept album on Atlantic Records. Other Wildhorn musicals in the works are *Carnivalle* (a Brazilian "Riverdance") written with Sergio Mendes and Jack Murphy, *Svengali* written with Gregory Boyd, the children's musical *Big Nose*, and the Gothic opera *Vampyr*. In the classical world, Wildhorn is currently developing the full-length ballet *Natasha*.

Jekyll & Hyde holds the distinction as the first new American musical to have two internationally released concept recordings of the score: *Highlights from Jekyll & Hyde* on RCA, and *Jekyll & Hyde—The Complete Work* on Atlantic Records. The latter's success launched a new label, Atlantic Theatre, of which Wildhorn is the Creative Director. Songs from *Jekyll & Hyde*, such as "Someone Like You," "A New Life," and "This Is The Moment," have been performed all over the world and have been used in the Olympics, the Superbowl, the World Series, the Miss America Pageant, and, most recently, at the 1996 Democratic National Convention and at the Inauguration (sung by Jennifer Holiday). *The Scarlet Pimpernel* score has already yielded it's own Top 40 Adult Con-

temporary hit with the song "You Are My Home," a duet recorded by Peabo Bryson and Linda Eder. Among the artists who have recorded and performed Wildhorn's music are Whitney Houston (the international Number One hit "Where Do Broken Hearts Go"), Natalie Cole, Kenny Rogers, Sammy Davis, Jr., Liza Minnelli, Julie Andrews, Freddie Jackson, Peabo Bryson, Trisha Yearwood, Deana Carter, Tracy Lawrence, John Berry, Trace Adkins, Betty Buckley, Ben Vereen, Regina Bell, The Moody Blues, Jeffrey Osborne, Jennifer Holiday, Stacy Lattisaw, Dennis DeYoung, Molly Hatchet, Brenda Russell, John Raitt, Anthony Warlow, Stanley Turrentine, Colm Wilkinson and Linda Eder, whose Atlantic debut album, *It's Time*, Wildhorn has written and co-produced.

Wildhorn is an associate artist in musical theatre with an endowed chair at the Alley Theatre in Houston, where he has launched *Jekyll & Hyde* and *Svengali* and has written music for Arthur Kopit's play *The Road To Nirvana* and scored the play *Cyrano de Bergerac*. Wildhorn enjoys a long-term relationship with Warner Bros. Pictures under the auspices of Lauren Schuler-Donner and Dick Donner where he is developing both feature-length musical animated films and live action musical projects as well.

As Creative Director of Atlantic Theatre for Atlantic Records, Wildhorn is helping develop both new American musical works and their potential stars, as well as building a bridge between the commercial theatre world and the music industry.

Lost In The Darkness

Words by Leslie Bricusse
Music by Frank Wildhorn

Moderately slow

Lost in the dark-ness, si-lence sur-rounds you. Once there was morn-ing, now end-less night. If I could reach you, I'd guide you and teach you to walk from the dark-ness back

into — the light.———————— Deep in your si - lence,

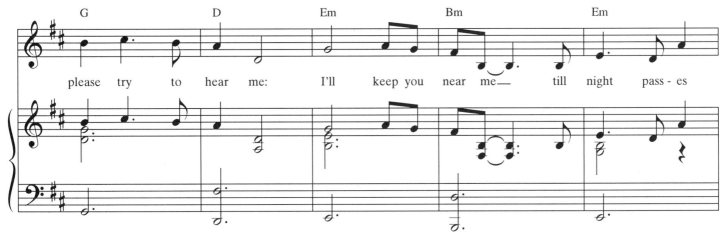

please try to hear me: I'll keep you near me— till night pass - es

by. I will find the an - swer. I'll nev - er de - sert you. I prom - ise you

this till the day that I die...————————

Façade

Words by Leslie Bricusse
Music by Frank Wildhorn

Fast

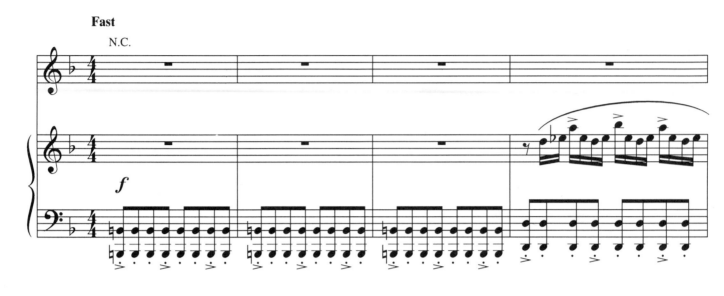

There's a

night-time ap-pears, and what's hid-ing in-side— be-hind all of our fears is our

true self,— locked in-side the fa-çade!————————

Ev - 'ry— day, peo - ple, in their own sweet— way,

like to add a coat of— paint— and be what they

18

cer - tain_ life is ter - ri - bly hard when your life's a fa - çade!

Look a - round you! I have found you can - not tell by look - in' at the sur - face what is lurk - in' there be -

neath it!

See that face! Now I'm pre - pared to bet you what you see's not what you

get 'cause man's a mas-ter of de - ceit! So what is this sin - is - ter se -

cret?_____ The lie he will tell you is true?_____ It's that

each man you meet— on the street is - n't one man, but two!_____

Near - ly ev - 'ry - one you see like him an' her an' you an' me pre -

tends to be a pil-lar of so-ci-e-ty,— a mod-el of pro-pri-e-ty, so-bri-e-ty an' pi-e-ty who shud-ders at the thought of no-to-ri-e-ty!— The la-dies and gents— 'ere be-fore you, which none of 'em ev-er ad-mits, may have saint-ly looks but they're sin-ners and crooks! Hyp-o-

23

cross if we could? Are we wait - ing— to break through the fa-

çade?— One or— two—

might look kind-a well - to - do,— hah! They're as bad as

me an'— you,— right down to their— boots!—

ev - er come clean, and the an - swer_ is it's all a fa -

çade, is it's all a fa - çade! Man is not one, but two. He is

e - vil and good, an' he walks the fine line we'd all

cross if we could! It's a night - mare_ we can nev - er dis -

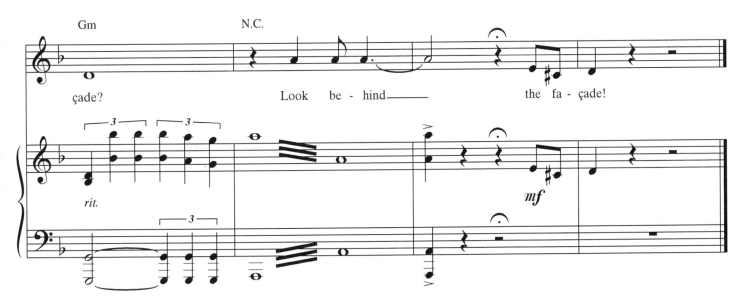

Take Me As I Am

Words by Leslie Bricusse
Music by Frank Wildhorn

Moderately slow

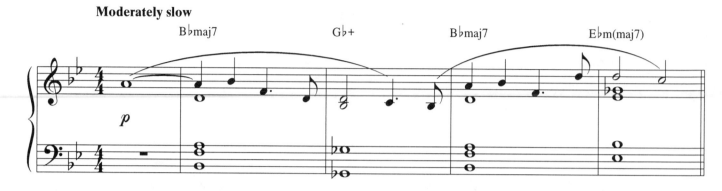

Jekyll: Some - times I see____ past the ho - ri - zon,
Emma: Look in my eyes,____ who do you see____ there?

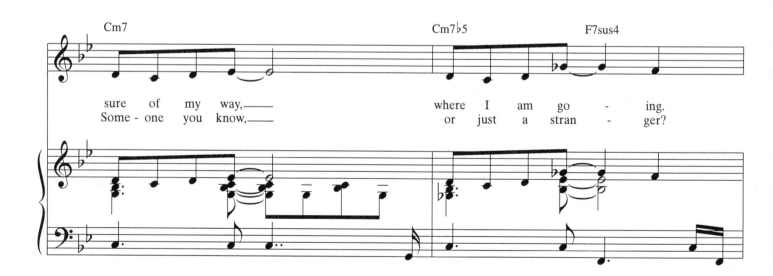

sure of my way,____ where I am go - ing.
Some - one you know,____ or just a stran - ger?

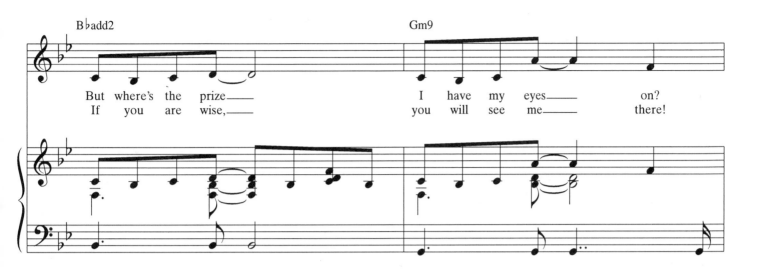

But where's the prize_____ I have my eyes_____ on?
If you are wise,_____ you will see me_____ there!

Where? There is just no know - ing! And when de - spair_____
Love is the on - ly dan - ger! Love, mean - ing me;_____

tears me in two,_____ who can I turn_____ to but you?_____
love, mean - ing you._____ We'll make that one_____ dream come true!_____

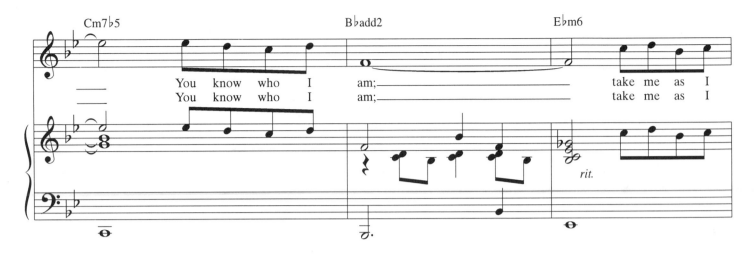

You know who I am;_____ take me as I
You know who I am;_____ take me as I

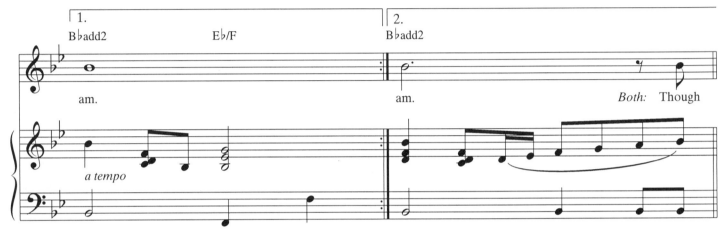

1. am.

2. am. *Both:* Though

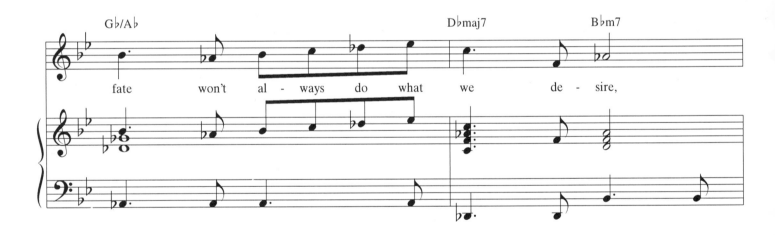

fate won't al - ways do what we de - sire,

still we can set the world on fire!

Give me your hand;— give me your heart.— *Jekyll:* Swear to me we'll— nev - er part!—

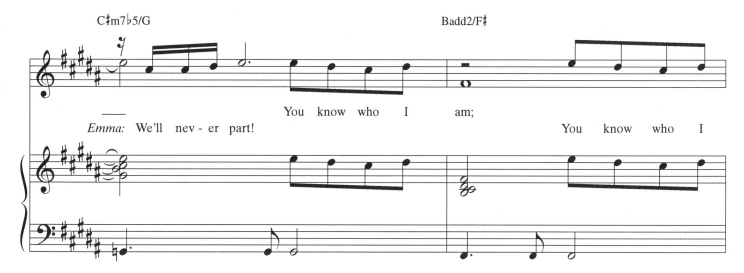

Emma: We'll nev - er part! You know who I am; You know who I

this is who I am. this is who I am.

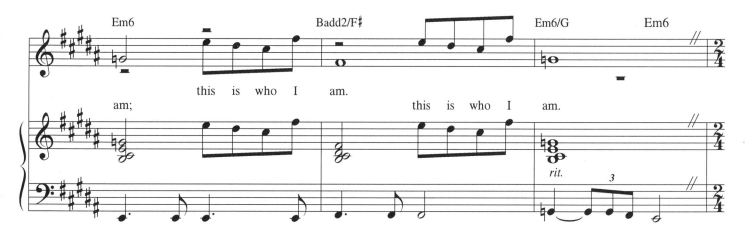

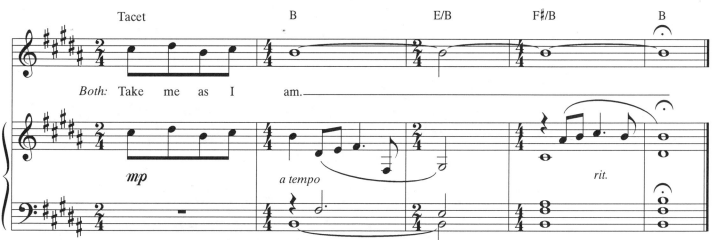

Both: Take me as I am.—

No One Knows Who I Am

Words by Leslie Bricusse
Music by Frank Wildhorn

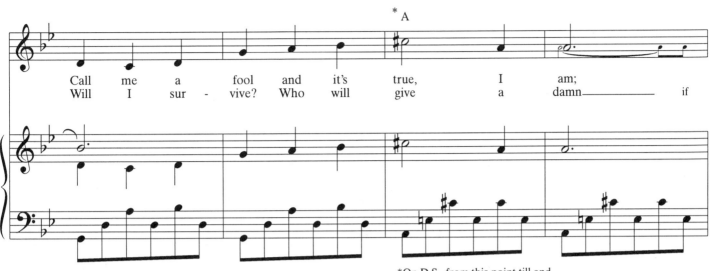

*A

Call me a fool and it's true, I am;
Will I sur-vive? Who will give a damn____ if

*On D.S., from this point till end,
play slowly and freely.

Cm   Gm

I don't know who I am.____
no one knows who I am?____

D7   Gm   D7   Gm

It's such a shame,   I'm such a sham.
No-bod-y knows,   not e-ven you.

No one knows who I am.
No one knows who I

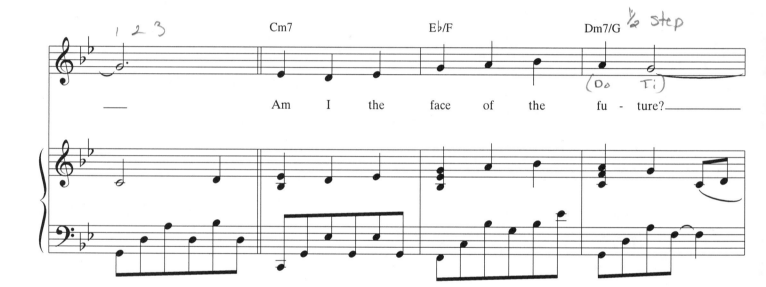

Am I the face of the fu - ture?

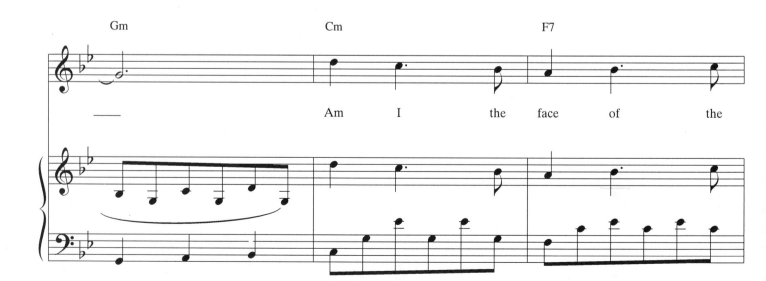

Am I the face of the

34

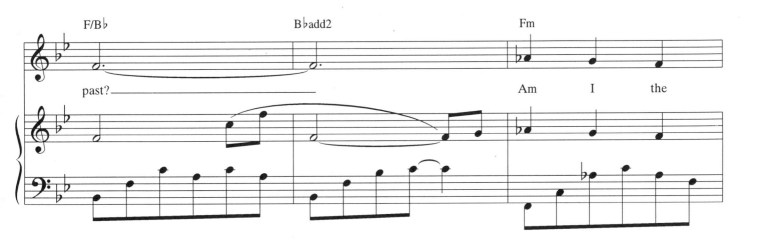

past?

Am I the

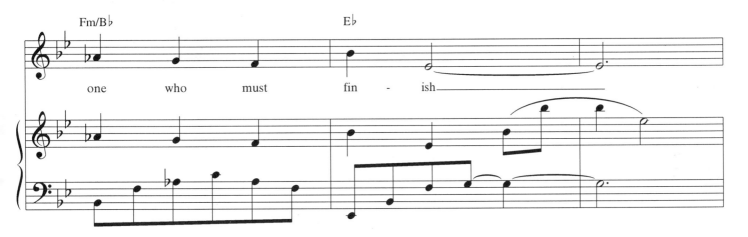

one who must fin - ish

D.S. al Coda

last?

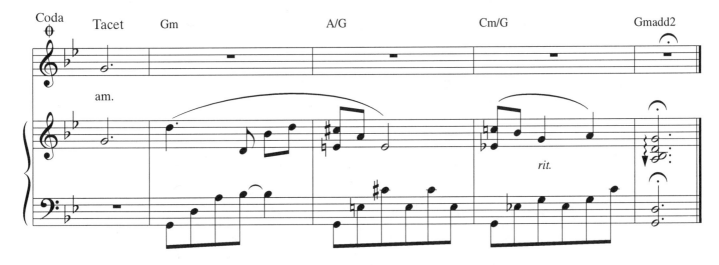

am.

rit.

Good And Evil

Words by Leslie Bricusse
Music by Frank Wildhorn

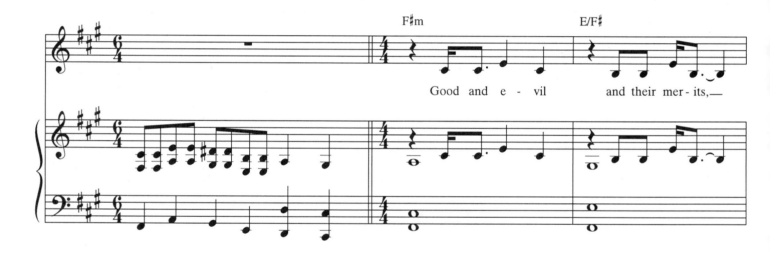

Bright jazzy 2

lose! But as I pe-ruse this world we a-buse,

it's hell that we choose, and heav-en must lose!_____

E-vil is ev-'ry-where, good does-n't have a prayer! Good is com-mend-a-ble,

e-vil's de-pend-a-ble! E-vil is vi-a-ble, good's un-re-li-a-ble! Good may be thank-a-ble!

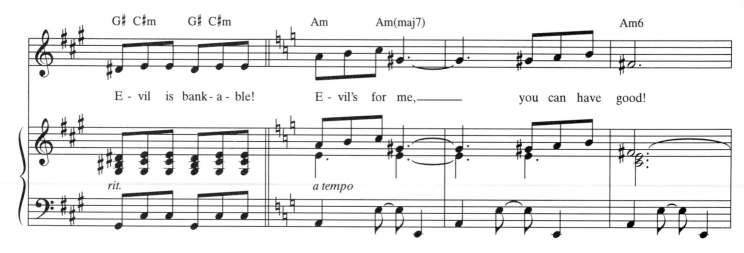

G♯ C♯m   G♯ C♯m   Am   Am(maj7)   Am6

E - vil is bank - a - ble! E - vil's for me,_____ you can have good!

rit.   *a tempo*

Am   Am(maj7)   Am6

Does - n't suit me_____ to be   Rob - in Hood!

F♯m7♭5   B7♭9

S'eas - ier by far, from the way that things are to re - main good and e - vil than

rit.

E7♭9♯5   Am   Am(maj7)   A5

try to be e - vil and good!_____

a tempo

This Is The Moment

Words by Leslie Bricusse
Music by Frank Wildhorn

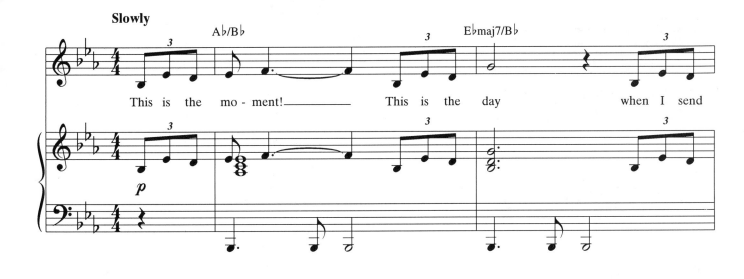

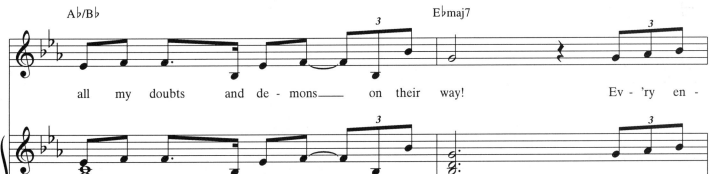

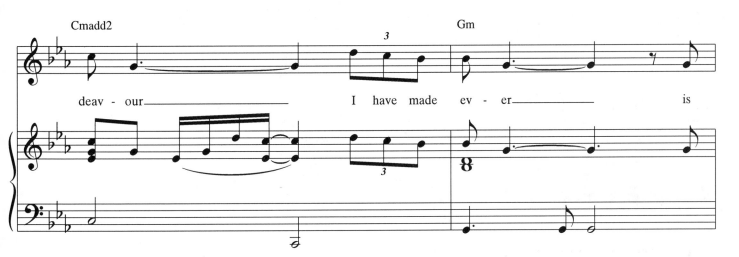

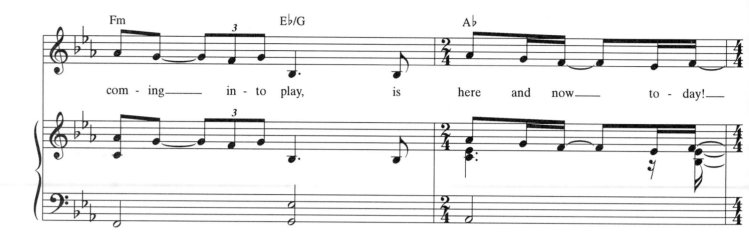

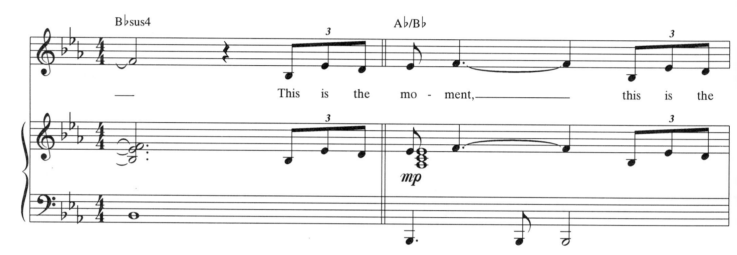

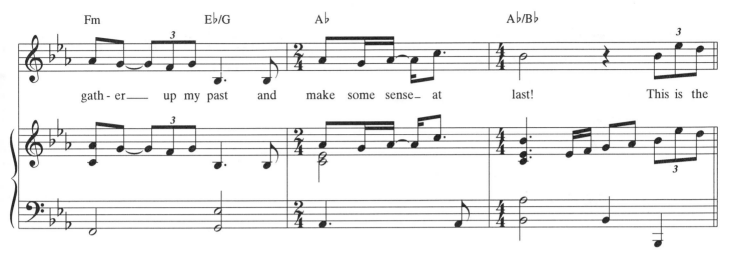

gath - er —— up my past and make some sense — at last! This is the

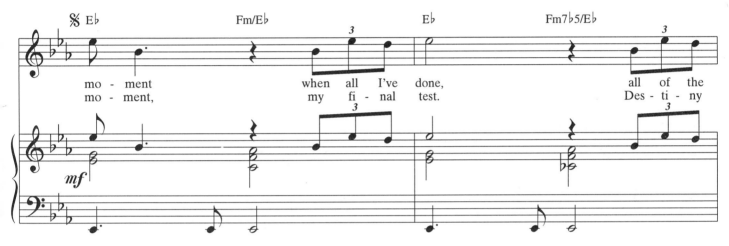

mo - ment, when all I've done,
mo - ment, my fi - nal test. all of the
Des - ti - ny

dream - ing, schem - ing and scream - ing be - come one! This is the
beck - oned, I nev - er reck - oned sec - ond best! I won't look

To Coda

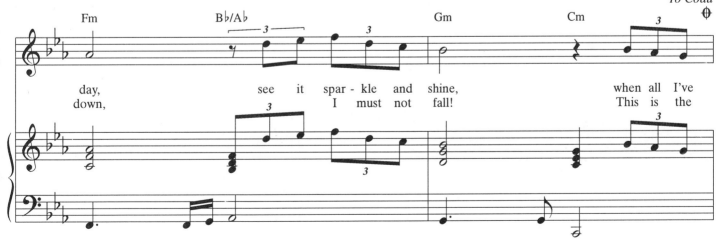

day, see it spar - kle and shine, when all I've
down, I must not fall! This is the

lived for_____ be - comes mine! For all these years I've

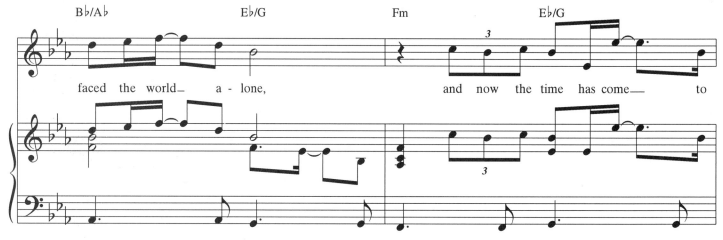

faced the world___ a - lone, and now the time has come___ to

D.S. al Coda

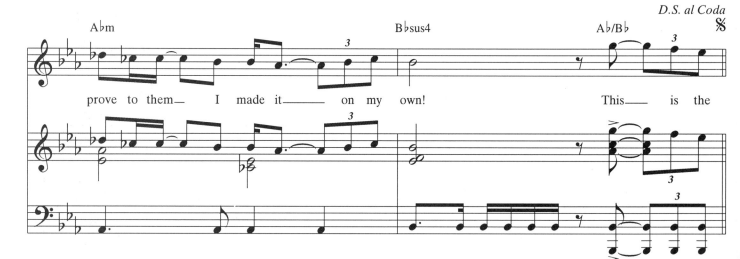

prove to them___ I made it_____ on my own! This___ is the

Coda

mo - ment, the sweet - est mo - ment of them all! This is the

Alive!

Words by Leslie Bricusse
Music by Frank Wildhorn

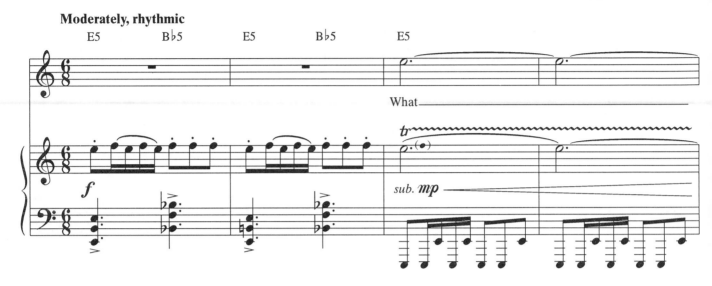

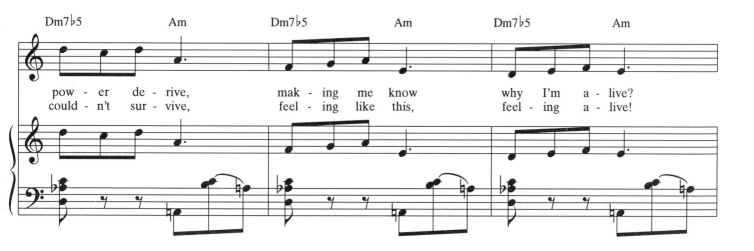

pow - er de - rive,   mak - ing me know   why I'm a - live?
could - n't sur - vive,   feel - ing like this,   feel - ing a - live!

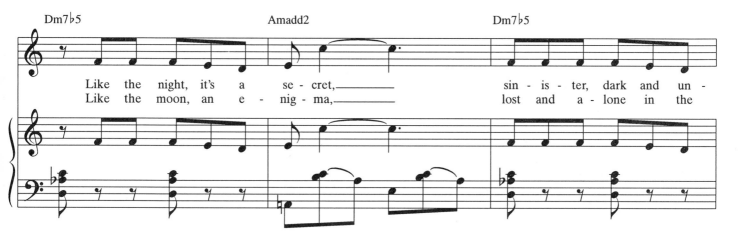

Like the night, it's a se - cret,   sin - is - ter, dark and un -
Like the moon, an e - nig - ma,   lost and a - lone in the

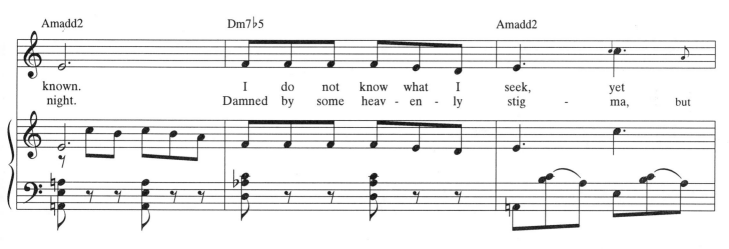

known.   I do not know what I seek,   yet
night.   Damned by some heav - en - ly stig - ma, but

I'll seek it a - lone!   blaz - ing   with

47

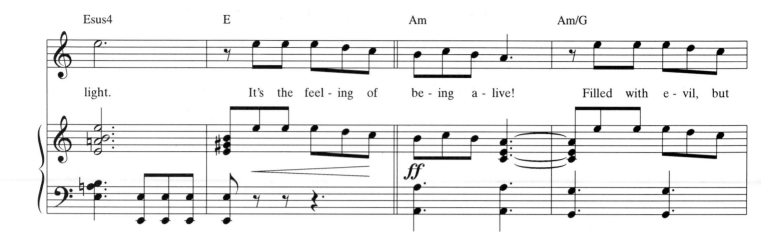

light.   It's the feel - ing of be - ing a - live!   Filled with e - vil, but

tru - ly a - live!   It's a truth that can - not be de - nied!   It's the feel - ing of

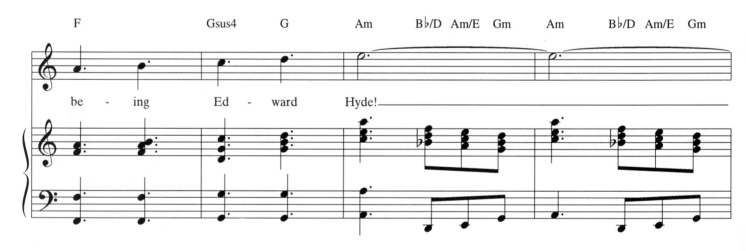

be - ing Ed - ward Hyde!

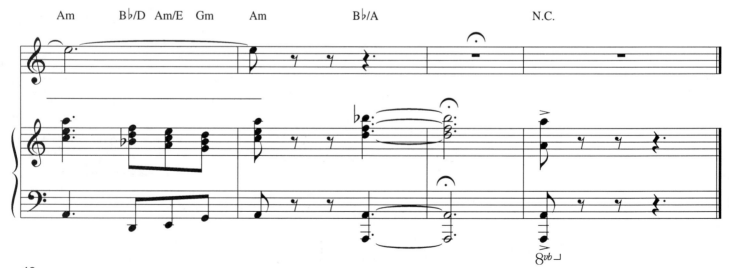

Sympathy, Tenderness

Words by Leslie Bricusse
Music by Frank Wildhorn

Moderately

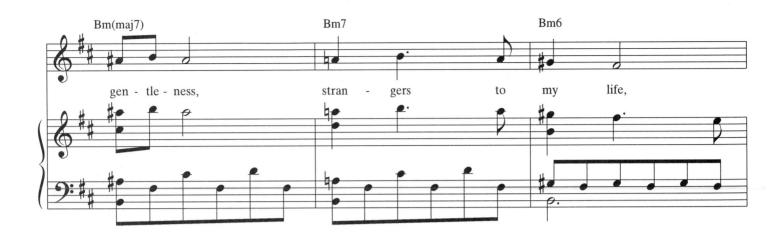

gen - tle - ness,   stran - gers   to   my   life,

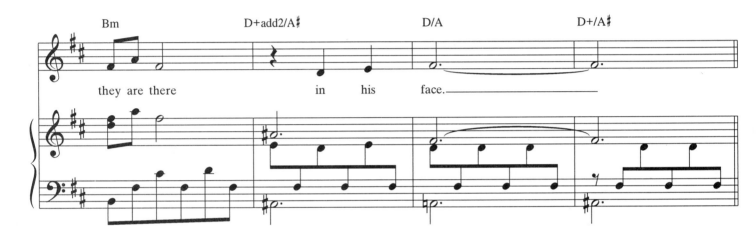

they are there   in   his   face.

Good - ness   and   sweet - ness   and   kind - ness   a -

bound   in   this   place.

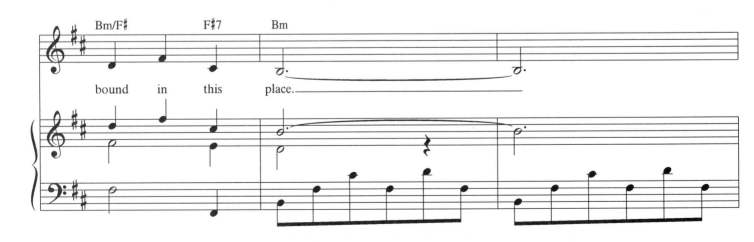

I am in love with the things that I

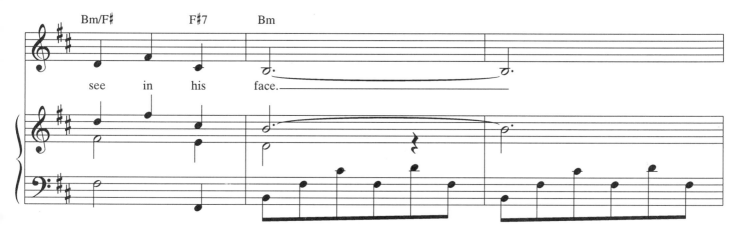

see in his face.

It's a mem-o-ry I know time will nev-er e-

rase.

Someone Like You

Words by Leslie Bricusse
Music by Frank Wildhorn

Slowly, freely

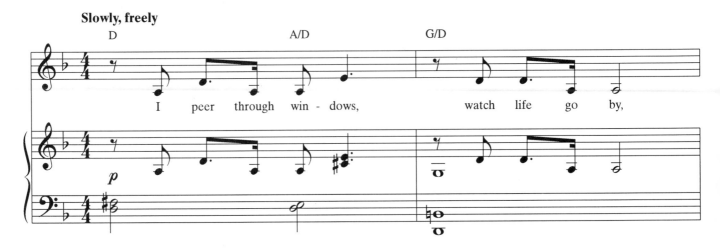

I peer through win - dows, watch life go by,

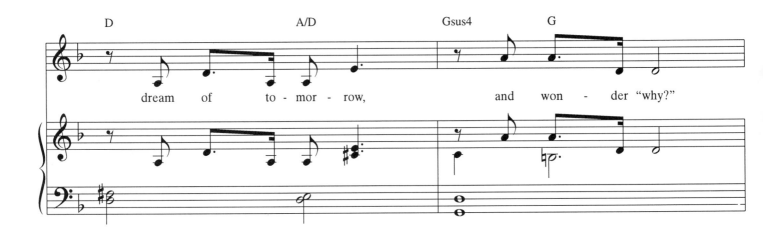

dream of to - mor - row, and won - der "why?"

The past is hold - ing me, keep - ing life at bay.

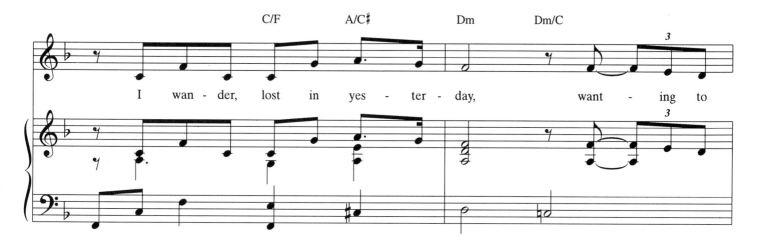

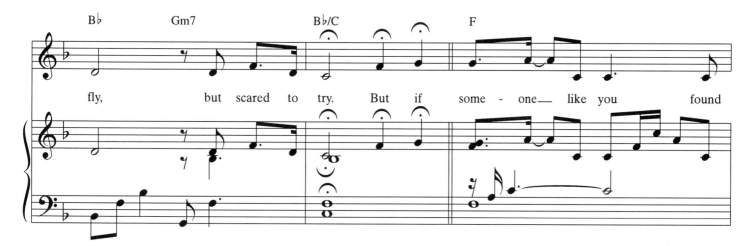

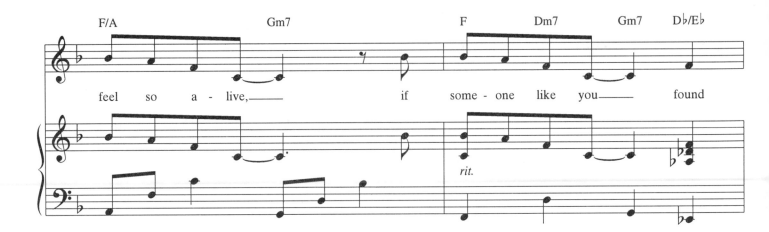

feel so a - live, ____ if some - one like you ____ found

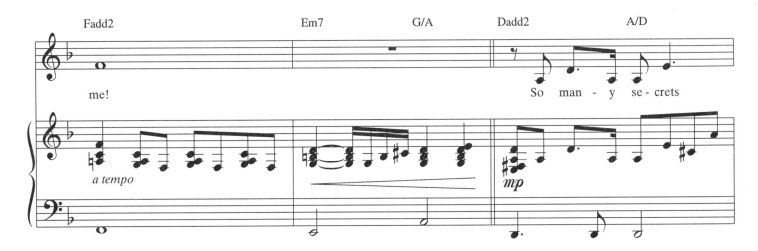

me! So man - y se - crets

I long to share! All I have need - ed

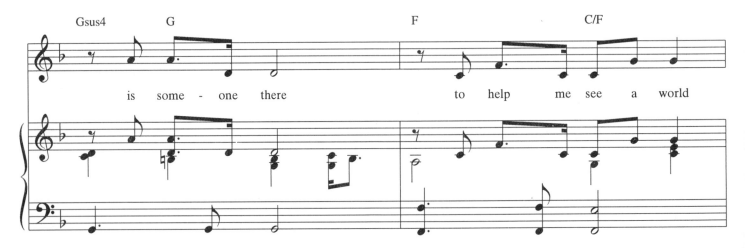

is some - one there to help me see a world

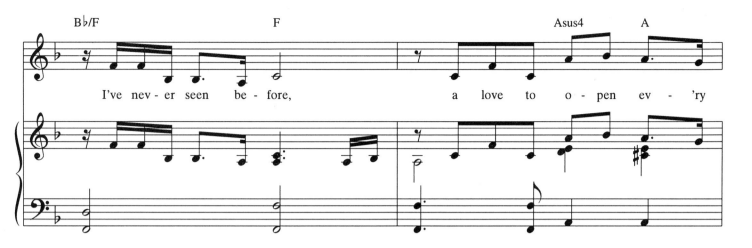

I've nev-er seen be-fore, a love to o-pen ev-'ry

door, to___ set me free so I can___

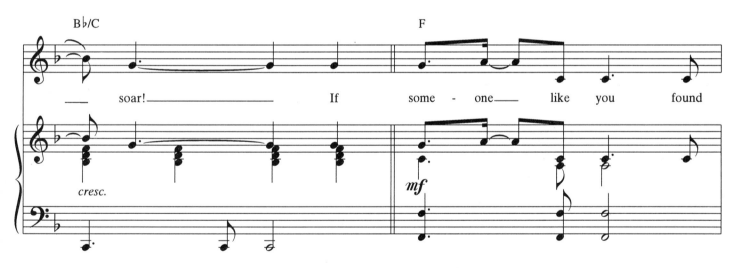

___ soar!_____ If some-one___ like you found

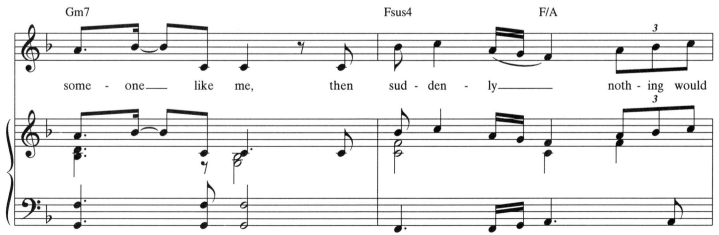

some-one___ like me, then sud-den-ly_____ noth-ing would

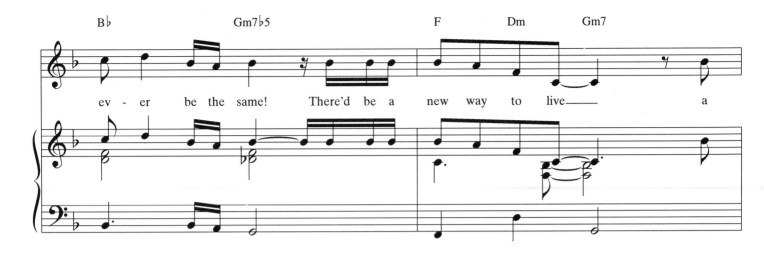

ev - er be the same! There'd be a new way to live___ a

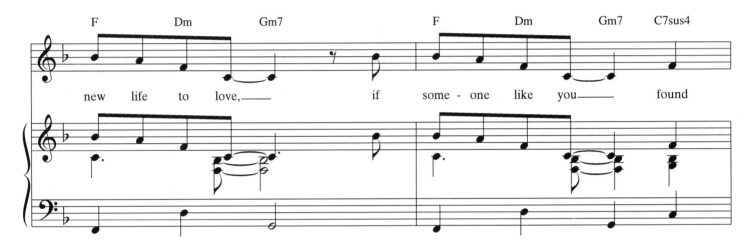

new life to love,___ if some - one like you___ found

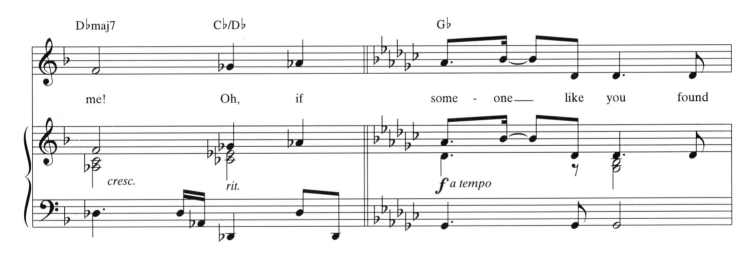

me! Oh, if some - one___ like you found

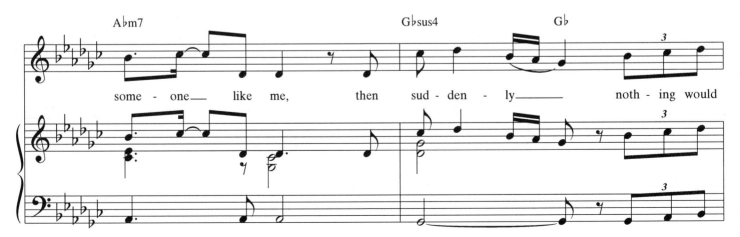

some - one___ like me, then sud - den - ly___ noth - ing would

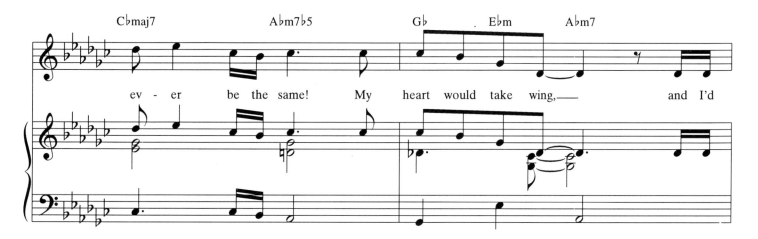

ev - er be the same! My heart would take wing,— and I'd

Slower, freely

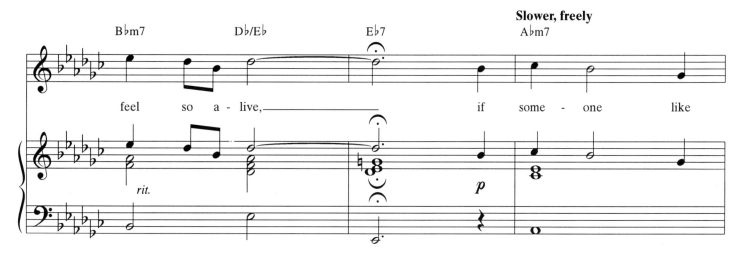

feel so a - live,— if some - one like

you loved me,— loved—

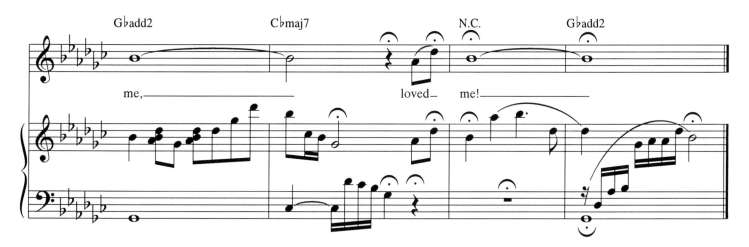

me,— loved— me!—

Murder, Murder!

Words by Leslie Bricusse
Music by Frank Wildhorn

a mo-ment prior to slaugh-ter! The shep-herd tend-in' to 'is flock!
The bloke what done it 'opped it! That fel-ler must be off 'is 'ead!

'E died in a Lon-don slum, a slave to mar-tyr-dom!
That's two in the last four days! This kill-er has fan-cy ways!

'E died with-out com-plaint! 'E should be made a saint! 'E's gone back 'ome to God!
To kill out-side St. Paul's re-quires a lot-ta balls! He hates the up-per class!

It all seems ver-y odd! Why should it be,
He must be on 'is arse! Who could he be?

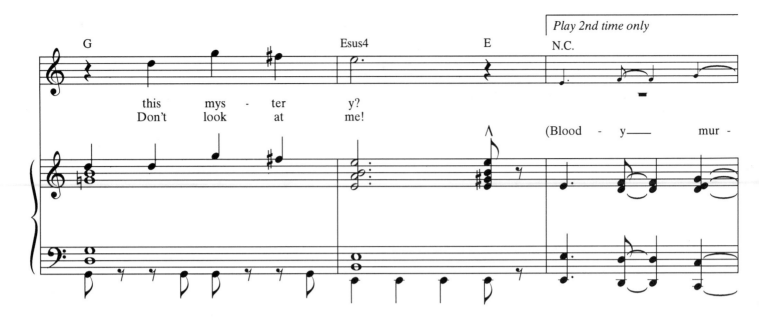

Play 2nd time only

this mys - ter - y?
Don't look at me!

(Blood - y—— mur -

Mur - der, mur - der, in the night air!
Mur - der, mur - der, do - in' night folks in!

der in the night.)——

Mur - der, mur - der, it's a night - mare! Mur - der, mur - der, it's a
Mur - der, mur - der is the worst sin! Mur - der, mur - der has me

A little slower

Sweet death has tak - en this brave man from us! Re - qui - em___ ae - ter - nam. Friends, take what com - fort that you can from us! Do - na e - is, Do - mi - ne...

They've got - ta try to nail him! They've got - ta trail an' jail him now! Mur - der!

No mat - ter who we're blam - in' till they pull wot's - 'is - name in,

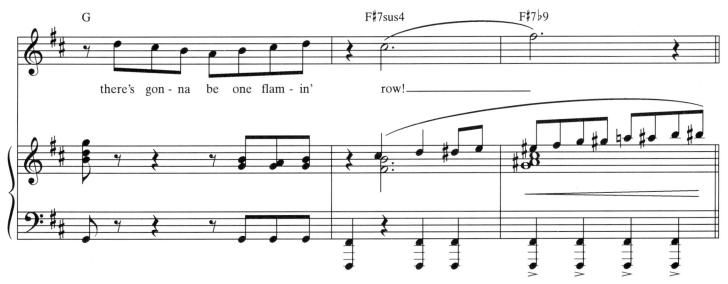

there's gon - na be one flam - in' row!

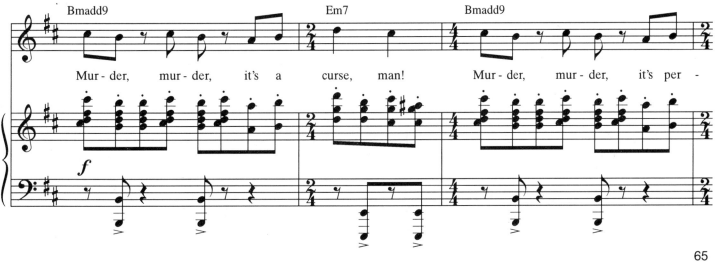

Mur - der, mur - der, it's a curse, man! Mur - der, mur - der, it's per -

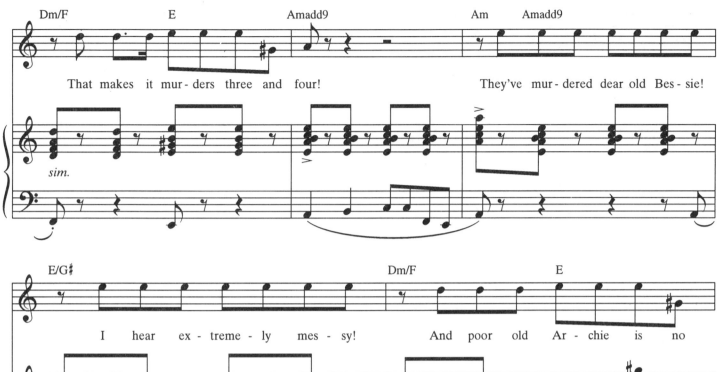

That makes it mur-ders three and four! They've mur-dered dear old Bes-sie!

I hear ex-treme-ly mes-sy! And poor old Ar-chie is no

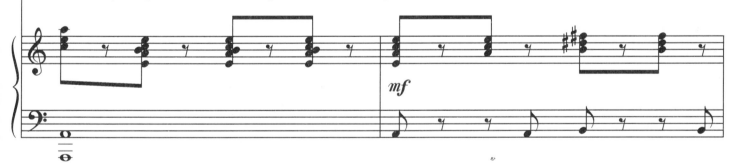

(Spoken:)
more! *They say a lot of blood an' gore!* That's four in the last eight days!

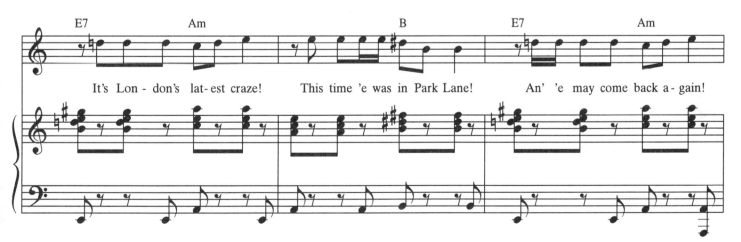

It's Lon-don's lat-est craze! This time 'e was in Park Lane! An' 'e may come back a-gain!

'Cos they're all so thick at Scot-land Yard! No brains!— No skill!

He'll kill us if we let him! They'd bet-ter go and get him!

I know a way to net him! How? Mur-der! No mat-ter who we're blam-in'

till they pull wot's-'is-name in, there's gon-na be, there's gon-na be, there's gon-na

one done, mur-der, mur-der can't be un-done! Mur-der, mur-der lives in

Lon-don! Blood-y mur-der in the night!_____ In the

night!_____

Once Upon A Dream

Words by Leslie Bricusse
Music by Frank Wildhorn

time ... like no oth - er time be - fore.

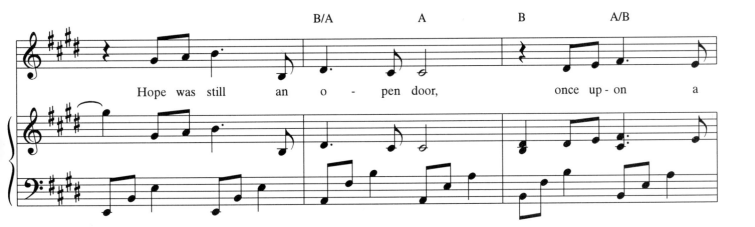

Hope was still an o - pen door, once up - on a

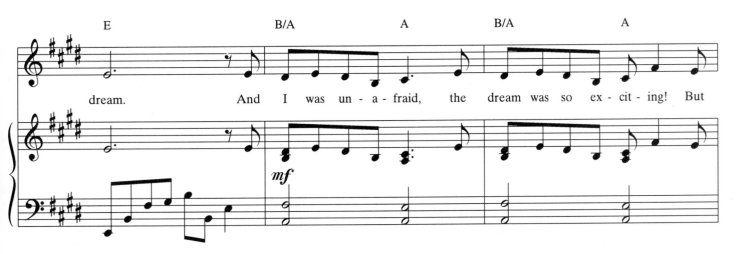

dream. And I was un - a - fraid, the dream was so ex - cit - ing! But

now I see it fade and I am here a - lone!

Once up-on a dream, you were heav - en

sent to me. Was it nev - er meant to be? Was it just a

dream? Could we be - gin a - gain,

once up - on a dream?

74

In His Eyes

Words by Leslie Bricusse
Music by Frank Wildhorn

Moderately, freely

with pedal

I sit and watch the rain and see my tears run down the win-dow-pane. I sit and watch the sky, and I can hear it breathe a sigh. I think of him, how we were. And when I

think of him, then I re - mem - ber, re - mem - ber...

Moderately, with a beat

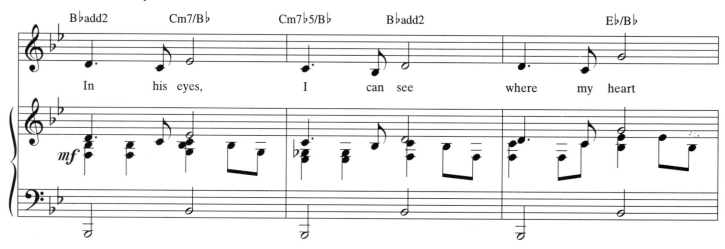

In his eyes, I can see where my heart

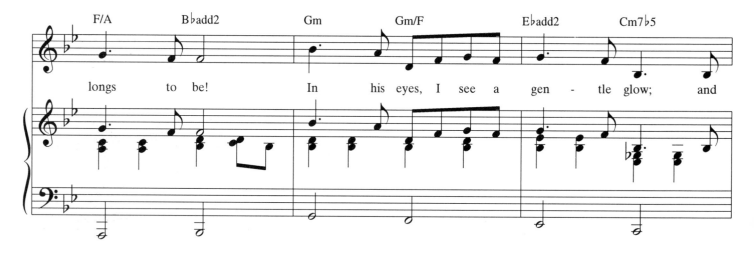

longs to be! In his eyes, I see a gen - tle glow; and

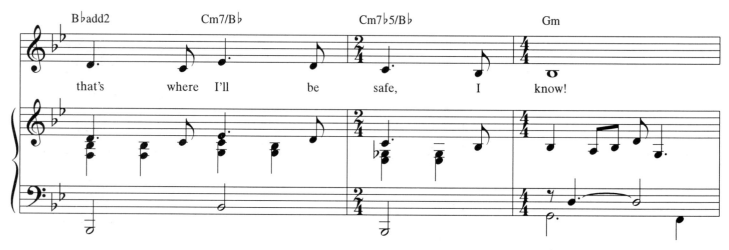

that's where I'll be safe, I know!

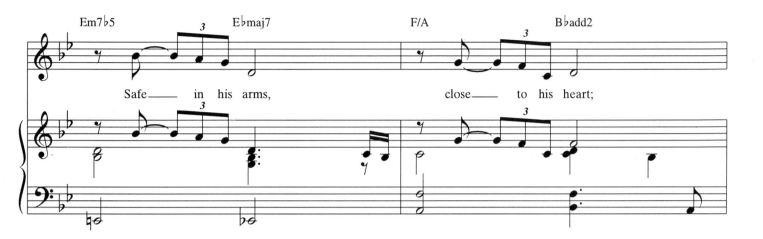

Safe—— in his arms, close—— to his heart;

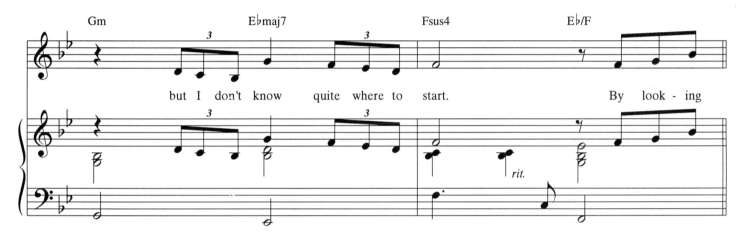

but I don't know quite where to start. By look - ing

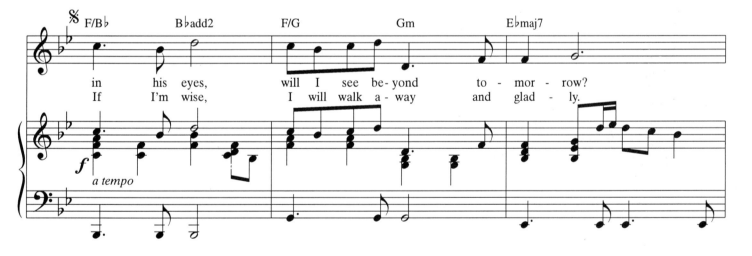

in his eyes, will I see be-yond to - mor - row?
If I'm wise, I will walk a - way and glad - ly.

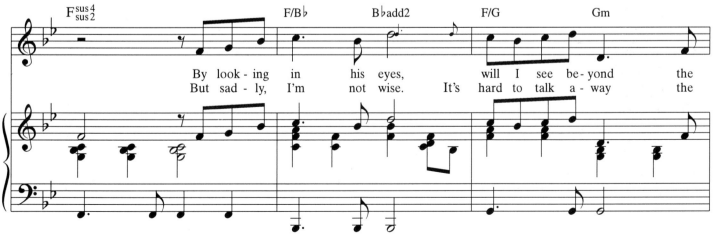

By look - ing in his eyes, will I see be-yond the
But sad - ly, I'm not wise. It's hard to talk a - way the

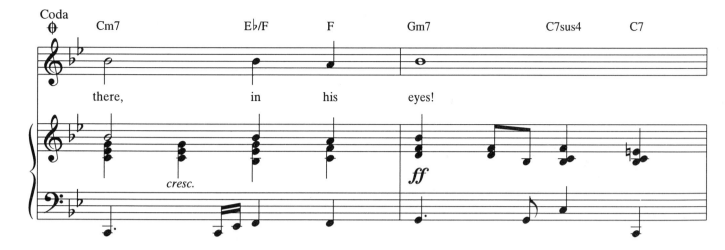

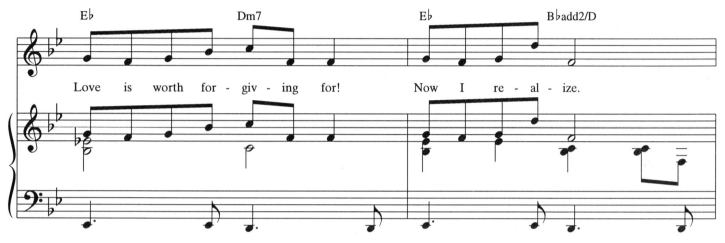

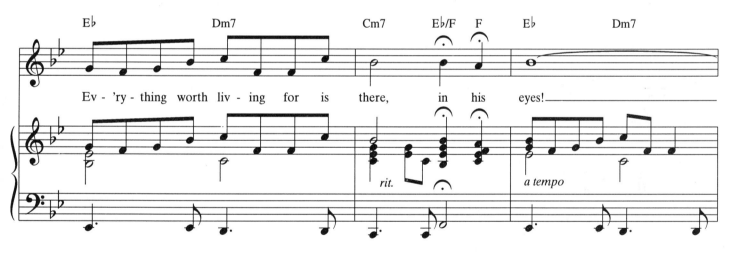

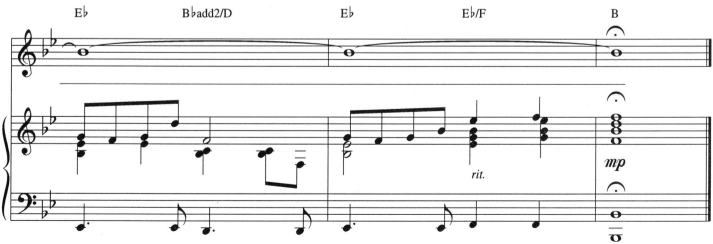

It's A Dangerous Game

Words by Leslie Bricusse
Music by Frank Wildhorn

I feel your fin - gers cold on my

shoul - der, your chill - ing touch as it runs down my

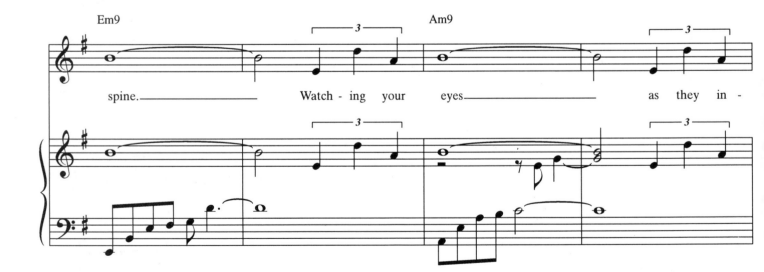

spine.____ Watch - ing your eyes____ as they in -

vade my soul, for-bid-den pleas - ures

I'm a-fraid to make mine.

Moderately fast

At the touch of your hand,_____ at the sound of your voice,_____
Will the ghost go a - way?_____ Will she will them to stay?_____

_____ at the mo - ment your eyes meet_____ mine, I am out of my mind,_____
_____ Ei - ther way, there's no way to_____ win! All I know is I'm lost_____

 end - ing,____ that's__ so un - real,____

you be - lieve__ that it's true!_____ A dance of death

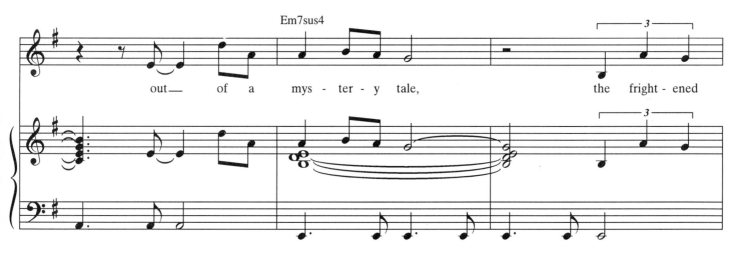

out__ of a mys - ter - y tale, the fright - ened

D.S. al Coda

prin - cess does - n't know what__ to do!_____

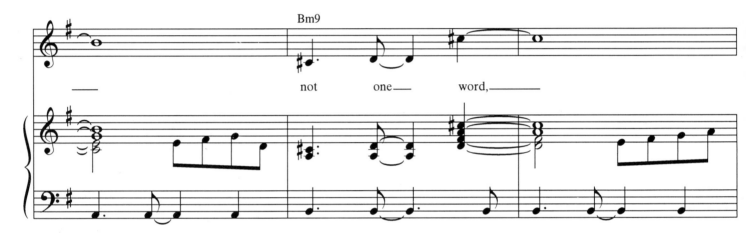

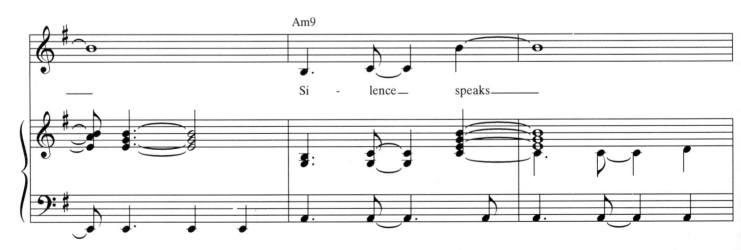

Gadd2   Am9

loud and— clear———   all the— words—

Bsus4

— we both want to hear.———————

rit.

Fm7   G7/F   B♭m/F

At the touch of your hand,— at the sound of your voice,— at the mo - ment your

a tempo

Fm   Fm7   G7/F

eyes meet— mine, I am los - ing my mind,— I am los - ing con - trol,—

85

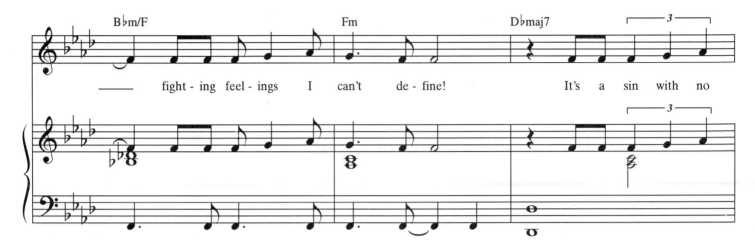

fight - ing feel - ings I can't de - fine! It's a sin with no

name, no re-morse and no shame,___ fire and fu - ry and flame 'cause the dev - il's to

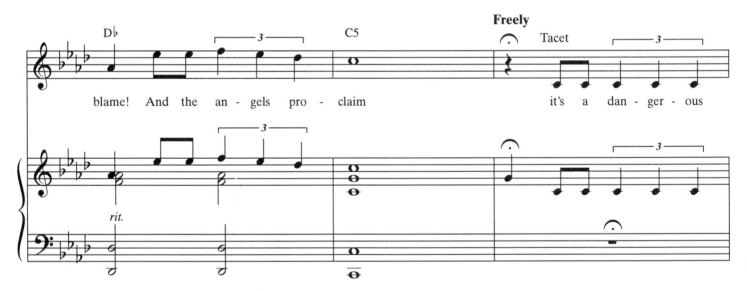

blame! And the an - gels pro - claim it's a dan - ger - ous

game!

A New Life

Words by Leslie Bricusse
Music by Frank Wildhorn

Moderately slow, freely

A new life, what I would-n't give to have a

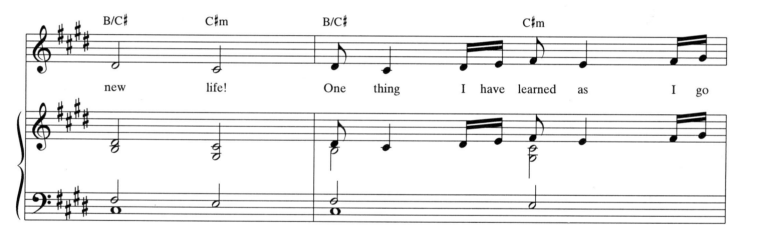

new life! One thing I have learned as I go

through life, noth-ing is for free a-long the way! A

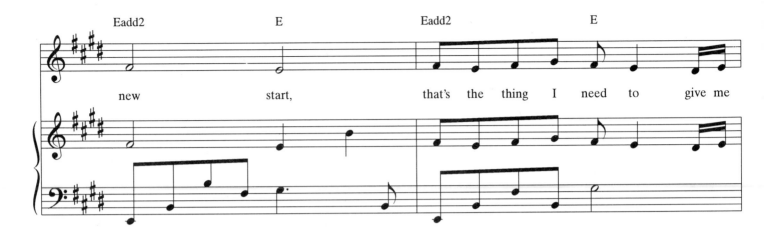

new start, that's the thing I need to give me

new heart. Half a chance in life_____ to find a

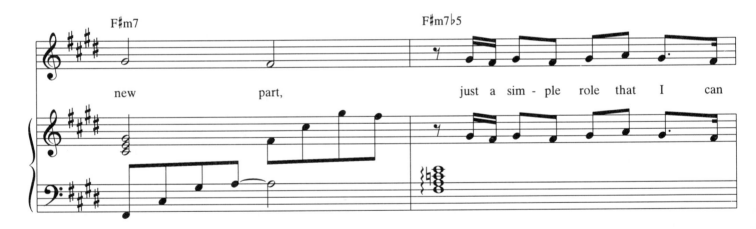

new part, just a sim - ple role that I can

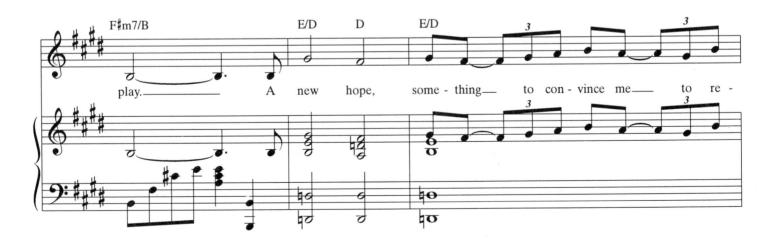

play._____ A new hope, some - thing_____ to con - vince me_____ to re-

Moderately, in rhythm

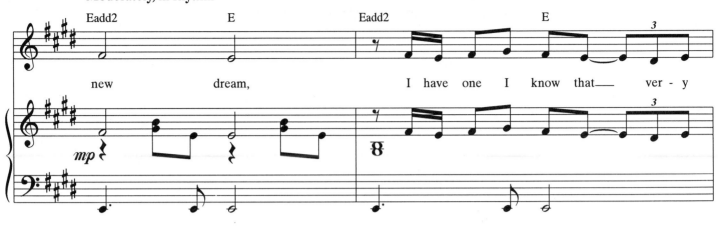

new dream, I have one I know that___ ver - y

few dream! I would like to see that___ o - ver -

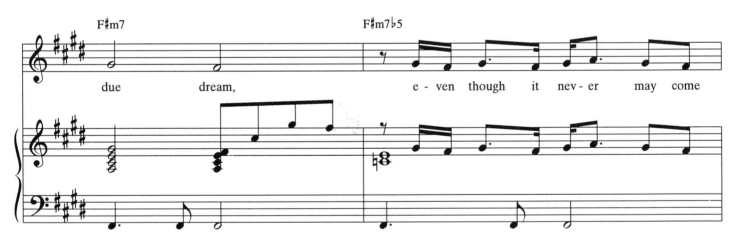

due dream, e - ven though it nev - er may come

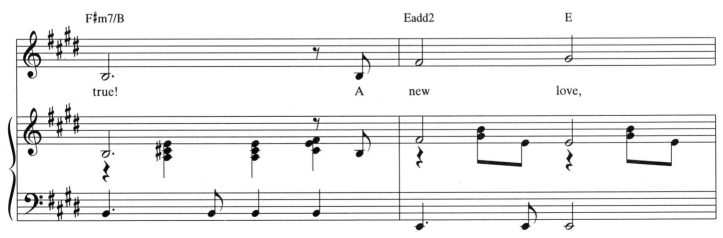

true! A new love,

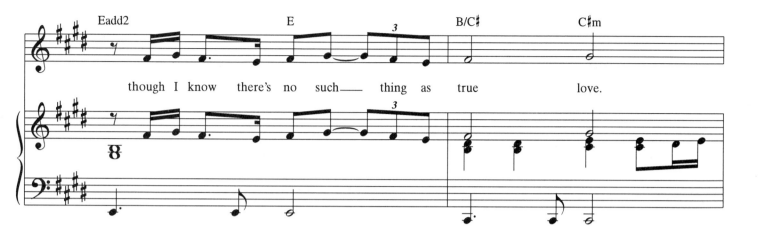

though I know there's no such___ thing as true love.

E - ven so, al - though I____ nev - er knew love,

still I feel that one dream_ is my due!

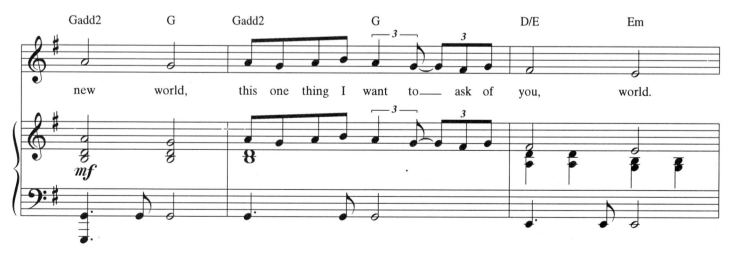

new world, this one thing I want to___ ask of you, world.

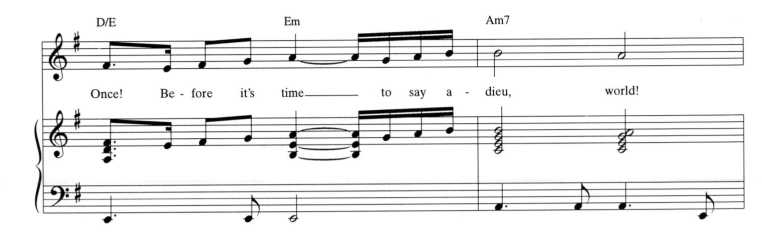

Once! Be - fore it's time_____ to say a - dieu, world!

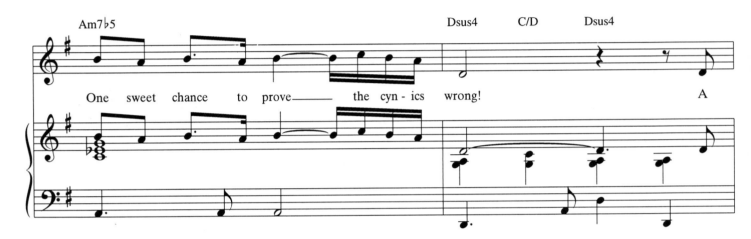

One sweet chance to prove_____ the cyn - ics wrong! A

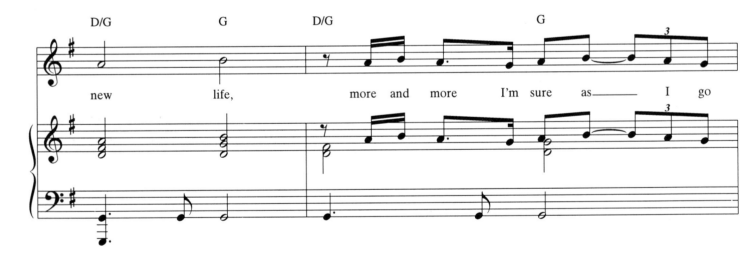

new life, more and more I'm sure as_____ I go through life.

Just to play the game and to pur -

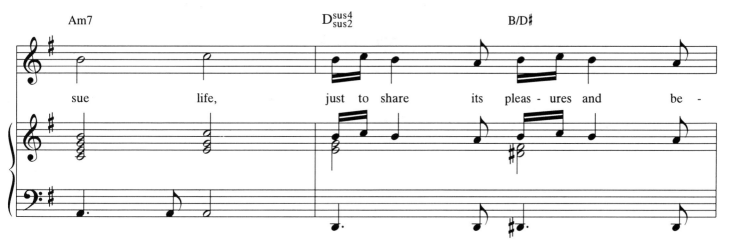

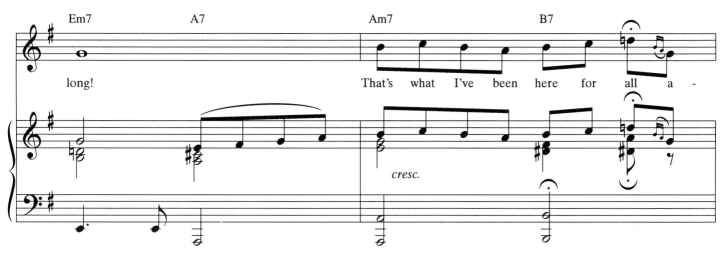

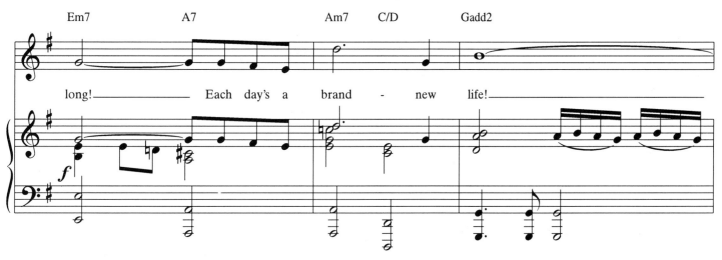

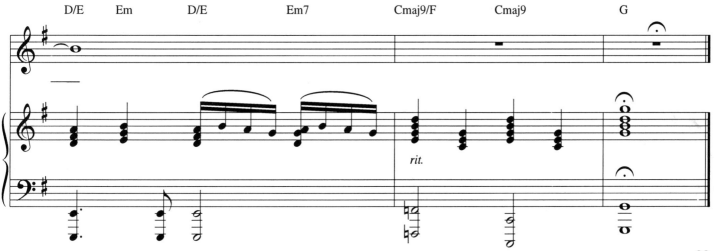

93

Confrontation

Words by Leslie Bricusse
Music by Frank Wildhorn

Moderately

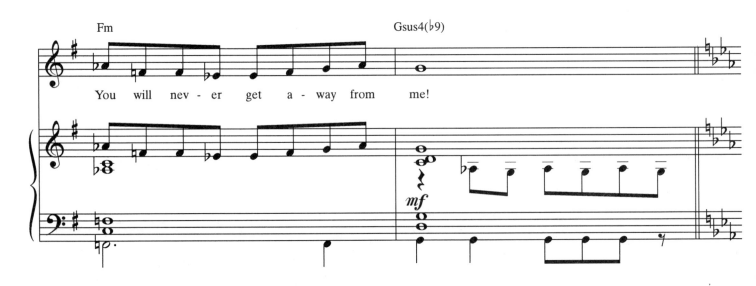

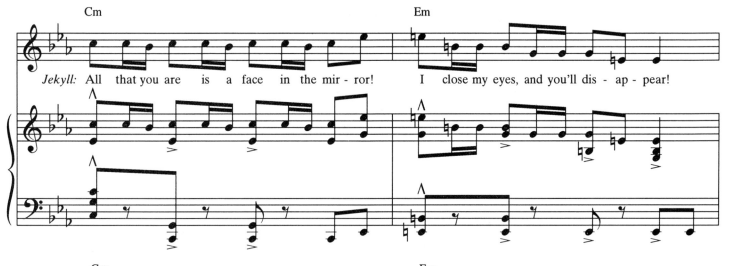

Cm   Em

Jekyll: All that you are is a face in the mir - ror! I close my eyes, and you'll dis - ap - pear!

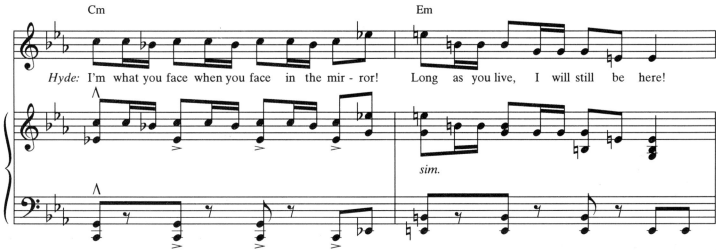

Cm   Em

Hyde: I'm what you face when you face in the mir - ror! Long as you live, I will still be here!

sim.

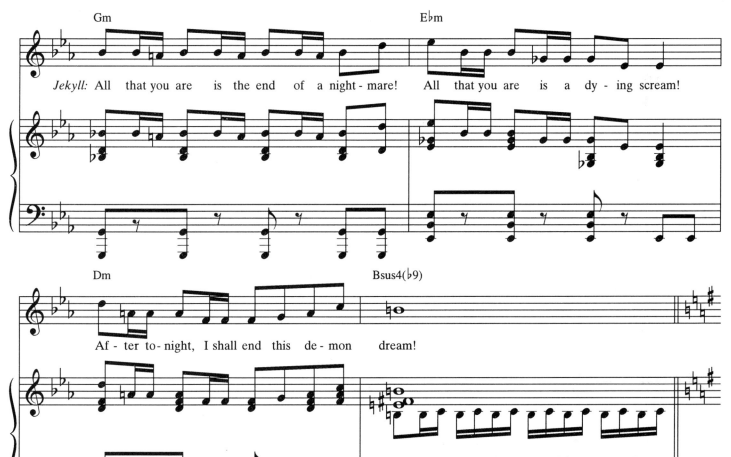

Gm   E♭m

Jekyll: All that you are is the end of a night - mare! All that you are is a dy - ing scream!

Dm   Bsus4(♭9)

Af - ter to - night, I shall end this de - mon dream!

Hyde: This is not a dream, my friend, and it will nev - er end!

This one is the night - mare that goes on!

Hyde is here to stay, no mat - ter what you may pre - tend,

and I'll flour - ish long af - ter you're gone!

Hyde: For I'll live in - side you for - ev - er! Jekyll: No!

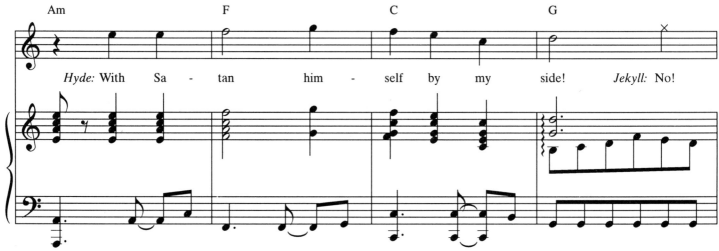

Hyde: With Sa - tan him - self by my side! Jekyll: No!

Hyde: And I know that, now and for - ev - er, they'll

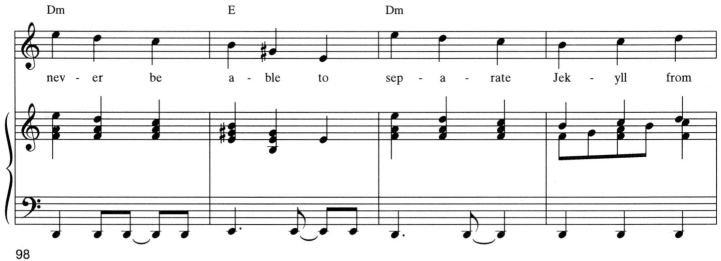

nev - er be a - ble to sep - a - rate Jek - yll from

98

100